# *Overcome Social Anxiety*

## *Methods to Liberate You from the Shackles of Social Anxiety*

# Blurb

We have all experienced some form of stress throughout our lives. Whether we felt our heartbeat increasing right before an important presentation, or felt very nervous before a first date, we all know how stress feels. Anxiety, however, is different – and it's much more exhausting to manage!

Social anxiety is a subset of generalized anxiety, and it is increasingly prevalent. In fact, with events like Covid-19, where we all stayed home and arguably forgot how to socialize after months of isolation, needless to say, many of us have become more anxious in social gatherings. And yet, while it may be used as a joke in many settings or on social media, social anxiety is far from being a laughing matter. Whether extremely severe or only experienced on certain occasions, social anxiety can quickly become overwhelming with time, especially as we engage in vicious cycles like the avoidance-anxiety mechanism.

But there is hope! *"Overcome Social Anxiety"* explores the various facets of social anxiety, outlining the common symptoms and triggers as well as the methods that can be used to overcome them. Upon reading this book, readers will understand what triggers their feelings of anxiety, what affects these triggers, and will find methods to help them cope with and overcome anxiety altogether. From CBT to skills training, "Overcome Social Anxiety" covers the ins-and-outs of social anxiety recovery, whether this is done independently or with the help of a psychologist.

# Contents

# Introduction

Most people know how stress feels: we have this pit in our stomach, we feel restless, and we might have physical symptoms too – we bite our nails, our heart rate increases, we may sweat more than usual, and we may even feel shaky in times of extreme stress. Stress is something that we experience all the time. Whether we have a big deadline coming up at work, a presentation to hold, or an important meeting that we need to attend and perform well in, we can all pinpoint moments in our lives where we felt the acute symptoms of stress. Anxiety, on the other hand, is something entirely different.

Anxiety is a feeling of unease, worry, or nervousness about something that could *potentially* happen. It usually is about something that is *going to happen*, or something that we do not completely understand. It comes up whenever an anxious person thinks about a situation that is uncertain. This means that anxiety can be a normal response to stress, such as when you have that big presentation coming, but it can also become an abnormal response to events that are *not* stressful, such as worrying so much about this presentation that you imagine all the potential worst-case scenarios that could potentially happen. You might stress so much about the presentation that you check whether you have your USB key eight times before you head over to the office. Or, you may be commuting and thinking about all the things that could go wrong – you will not show up at the right room, you misread the starting time, you might trip and fall on your way up… And while these are all *potential scenarios,* they are unlikely to happen, yet still feel them as events that are likely to happen. Anxiety is particularly different from stress because it can begin to interfere with your daily activities, and hence, it can cause significant distress.

Within the large realm of anxiety, we also find *social* anxiety. Social anxiety particularly refers to a fear, or an intense phobia that is associated with social situations. You may fear being embarrassed, judged, or even scrutinized by people around you. You may imagine that when you walk into the room, everyone is looking at you and thinking about what you are wearing, what you are doing there, why you are there, and the like. There are situations in which you are more prone to social anxiety, such as when you need to give a big speech, or when you are indeed the center of attention. In other situations however, such as mundane ones like going to the bathroom in public, feeling intensely scared or worried is considered anxiety. As such, the bottom line is the following: if you are worried because you know the risks are true – for example, you are worried about your presentation because this is the first time you are giving one in a new company and you are the youngest new hire – then this is normal anxiety. On the other hand, if you are anxious about going to the bathroom because you are worried that someone may say something humiliating to you while you have no grounds to believe so (something we call "evidence" in the world of anxiety), then you are most likely experiencing social anxiety.

Social anxiety disorder is a treatable condition, and people with this condition can benefit from various forms of treatment, including cognitive-behavioral therapy, medication, and lifestyle changes. With proper treatment, you can overcome your fears and lead fulfilling lives, free of the restraints and shackles of anxiety. This is precisely the goal of this book – to give you the information and tools you need to gain control over your feelings of anxiety and to be empowered throughout the process. With this in mind, this book has thoughtfully been broken down into two core sections. First, section one outlines what social anxiety is specifically, including the core symptoms to look out for, the impacts it can have on daily life, as well as the cycle of avoidance and anxiety. Second, section two looks at techniques to manage social anxiety so you can be well on your way to recovery.

It's time to take back control. Get ready for a life-changing book!

# Section One: Uncovering Social Anxiety

In this section, we look at the key causes and triggers of social anxiety, the types of social anxiety, as well as its symptoms. We will furthermore be exploring the impact that social anxiety can have on daily life and the cycle of avoidance and anxiety. To break this cycle and give you control over your life again, we need to talk about things the way they are! So, let's uncover the facets of social anxiety.

# Chapter One:
## Understanding Social Anxiety

In simple terms, social anxiety refers to the kind of anxiety that one feels when they are extremely fearful of social situations. These can be any kind of situation ranging from going to the bathroom in public, to showing up on your own to a party, or speaking in public. The key point to remember is that this is something you have control over. In other words, it is something that you can work on by using the tips and tricks, as well as the kinds of therapies that are outlined in this book.

Often, a key question asked about social anxiety is where it originates from. Unfortunately, the specific reasons for social anxiety are not well-understood yet, and they require more research. However, the science so far suggests that there are a few factors that may influence the emergence of social anxiety in individuals. It has been suggested that genetic, environmental, and psychological factors are in part responsible for social anxiety. This may explain why, for example, a person with a family history of anxiety disorders (e.g., your mother being prescribed anxiety medication), or childhood experiences such as being bullied in high school, may lead you to develop social anxiety later on in life.

When suffering from social anxiety, you are likely to experience **triggers**. These refer to the specific events or situations that stimulate a response, such as an anxiety attack or symptoms of anxiety, which will be discussed shortly. Triggers are important to recognize as this is a crucial step in understanding how *you* operate as someone with anxiety. The more you understand yourself, your reactions, your feelings and what makes you "tick," the more aware you are of what you can do to avoid feeling this way. Triggers can range from speaking in public to simply meeting new people, but they include other experiences, such as going to large events, where you may feel especially self-conscious or nervous about having to make small talk with people. You may be extremely worried about what they will think of you, what opinion they will have, what response they will have to what you have to say, and the like. Such large events are common triggers of social anxiety, so if you feel that it is one of yours, don't worry – you aren't alone.

Another common trigger is being the center of attention. Think about the following scenario: it is your birthday and you have kindly asked your friends not to organize any kind of "happy birthday" singing because having all eyes on you is your very own version of hell. However, as you see your friend getting up to use the bathroom, you also see her speaking to one of the waitresses, whispering in her ear and trying to not-so-subtly point at you. How do you feel? Do you feel like the color has drained from your face? Like you suddenly are struggling to breathe? Are a million thoughts running through your head, such as *what will people around us think? They're going to be so annoyed. Oh God, everyone will be looking at me, I'm going to get so red, and everyone will laugh at me. What if my friends are doing this to embarrass me?"* If so, this may be a trigger for you.

Other common triggers include more specific experiences, such as eating in public or speaking to authority figures. The former is especially the case for people who may have body image issues, as they may be extremely worried about what others may think of them as they eat in public. Or, they may worry about being judged for their eating habits, choking or spilling food and embarrassing themselves, or attracting unwanted attention. Likewise, speaking to authority figures may be intimidating, whether this is a boss, a teacher, or a police officer – the thought of doing so may be enough to trigger a full-blown panic attack.

Before you head over to the next chapter, take some time to think about what your triggers might be. Have you ever felt uneasy in social situations? Can you pinpoint which part of the situation made you feel uneasy?

# Chapter Two:
## Symptoms of Social Anxiety

Social anxiety can manifest itself differently depending on the person. Generally-speaking, however, it has common symptoms that you may have experienced in the past, or even recently. Throughout this chapter, we will be exploring common symptoms of anxiety to help you pinpoint which ones may be troubling you the most, and hence, to help you prepare how you can overcome them in the next section.

First, there is the **fear of being judged, criticized, or rejected by others.** When we feel anxious in social situations, we typically focus on what others are thinking. *Will they judge my dress? What if I dressed too casually, or too business-like! That girl in the background is definitely giving me a side eye. What* *will my boss think?!* And the thoughts keep on running. You may think of all the scenarios that could happen, such as what would happen if you said something wrong, or what could happen if you made a wrong move in said social occasion. You may even think about what might happen if you show up, and no one's there – rejection hurts, and this possibility, although very very unlikely (something you may even know rationally!) is still worrying! Remember, stress is different from anxiety – if you have felt like this on a singular occasion, it may not be anxiety. If you cannot attend social functions without feeling this way, however, you may indeed be dealing with social anxiety.

Second, there is the **avoidance of social situations or people**. This is particularly the case for generalized social anxiety disorder, which is one of two common types of social anxiety (the other being social phobia, which is where you fear specific social situations, such as eating in front of people, but do not experience others, like using public restrooms). Do you ever find yourself avoiding situations so as not to be stuck in a situation where you feel anxious? For example, do you ever skip a party because you are worried about what others will think? Or do you self-sabotage by calling in sick on the day you are due to be giving a speech?

Third, there is **intense anxiety and nervousness in social situations**. If you do indeed attend such situations, you may nevertheless loathe the entire process. You may feel extremely unwell or uncomfortable, and may be counting down the minutes until it is appropriate for you to leave having shown up and said hello to people. This may also be accompanied by physical symptoms, like sweating, trembling, blushing, or feeling like your heart rate is through the roof.

Other symptoms include struggling to speak with others or making eye contact with people, which could be reinforced by deep self-consciousness and self-doubt as well as negative thoughts and self criticism, such as thoughts like *"I'm going to sound like an idiot if I speak"* or *"this person thinks I'm full of it"*. In severe cases, you might have a panic attack.

These symptoms, as you may know, are extremely uncomfortable to deal with. Social anxiety can impact your daily life by leading you to withdraw from your social circles because of these overwhelming feelings of worry and self-criticism, and they may end up affecting both your personal and professional relationships. Social anxiety can affect job performance, such as in cases where you can't give presentations or speak in public, or if you can't network. Then, it can lead to a vicious cycle, namely that of avoidance and anxiety. Let's explore this in more detail.

# Chapter Three:
## The Cycle of Avoidance and Anxiety

Those who struggle with anxiety tend to fall into a vicious cycle of avoidance that only reinforces their anxiety. The cycle of avoidance and anxiety begins with a **trigger**, which is a situation or interaction that causes anxiety, as mentioned in a previous chapter. For example, imagine you are invited to a party. The thought of going to the party makes you feel nervous and anxious. This party makes you have all kinds of thoughts – *what will people think of my job? What if my friends don't show up? I'm scared people will judge me because I've gained weight. There is no point in going if I'm going to feel bad about it...*

These are the thoughts that lead to avoidance behaviors, which are **actions that you take to avoid the trigger.** In this case, you may decide not to go to the party or make up an excuse to avoid it – *"So sorry! I'm drowning in work. Catch up next week?"*. This avoidance behavior provides temporary relief from anxiety, but it reinforces the belief that the situation is dangerous or threatening. You may not feel it right away, but by constantly allowing your brain to avoid the anxiety-inducing trigger, you are effectively teaching yourself that these are, indeed, dangerous situations. But as we have seen throughout this book, this is not the case. In fact, in most cases, there is no danger at all – but our brain convinces us otherwise.

Over time, these avoidance behaviors can become entrenched, leading to the shrinking of your comfort zone. For example, if you consistently avoid parties, you may start to feel anxious about other social situations, such as going out to dinner with friends or attending a work event. Suddenly, things that never caused anxiety before start to trigger symptoms, which is confusing but is only reinforced by more avoidance behaviors.

This cycle of avoidance and anxiety can be worsened by negative thoughts and self-criticism – all the negative self-talk you do (*What will they think of me? They are all judging me. No one actually likes me as their friend, they only pity me…*). You may tell yourself that you are not good enough, that people will judge or reject you, or that you will embarrass yourself.

These negative thoughts can reinforce the belief that the trigger is dangerous or threatening, leading to more anxiety in the future, and giving you more reasons to continue the cycle.

But it can be broken! Breaking the cycle of avoidance and anxiety requires a willingness to face your fears and challenge your negative thoughts, which is what we will do in the following section.

# Section Two: Breaking the Cycle to Overcome Anxiety

The cycle of avoidance and anxiety can feel like you are perpetually stuck, but this is just another negative thought to learn to control. You can choose to expose yourself to anxiety-inducing moments to stop feeding the anxious monster inside of you. Throughout the next few pages, we will be having a look at exactly how you can do this, namely by exploring the various kinds of therapies and training that you can do.

# Chapter Four:
## Cognitive Behavioral Therapy

Starting out with Cognitive Behavioral Therapy, or more commonly known as CBT, this kind of therapy has been particularly helpful when it comes to reframing the thoughts that support anxious feelings. Specifically, CBT reframes how we think by pushing us to find evidence for the feelings we have. If you feel anxious, you are encouraged to look around you, look at your past experiences, and the like to figure out whether or not these anxious thoughts are rooted in your beliefs – which are not always true, and usually based on fears instead of facts – or whether they are indeed true. Specifically, CBT helps you identify and change negative thought patterns as well as behaviors that are contributing to your feelings of anxiety and other problems you may be dealing with.

CBT is based on the principle that the ways in which we think, feel, and hence behave are all interconnected. Thus, if we change one of these elements, the other two also change along with it. For example, if you change the thoughts that enable the cycle of avoidance and anxiety, your actions change along with it.

CBT is done in various ways. For example, it involves **cognitive restructuring,** which is where you identify and challenge the negative thoughts you have. So, if you think *"I'm going to embarrass myself!"* when deliberating whether or not to go to a party you've been invited to, you are prompted to think – what evidence do I have for this belief? What experiences have I had in the past that show me that this would happen? Then, you start working on these thoughts by making them more positive, such as by saying *"It's good for me to see friends and socialize. My friends like me, and I enjoy their company."* By focusing on positivity, you slowly teach your brain to dissociate the negative thoughts from the experience, instead focusing on the positive aspects of the situation.

You don't need to work with a psychologist to try out CBT. In fact, there are tons of worksheets online that can help you tremendously! Check them out and see if they help.

# Chapter Five:
## Exposure Therapy

Ah, exposure therapy – the kind of solution to the avoidance-anxiety cycle that so many detest! And yet, it is also one of the most effective ways to deal with anxiety and to break the cycle head-on. Exposure therapy is exactly what the name suggests: you expose yourself to your triggers, slowly and little by little, so you gain more confidence throughout the process and feel empowered as a result. The more you expose yourself to these situations, the more you force your brain to change the way it perceives these experiences as anxiety-inducing. Gradually, you feel less anxious when thinking about situations that you would have previously avoided at all costs.

An easy example of this is speaking to a stranger at a café. Now, naturally, if you are extremely anxious, this may be very anxiety-inducing. In such a case, it may be best to start with a smaller step, such as by speaking to the barista and asking them how they are doing today. On the other hand, if you feel like speaking to a stranger is easy to do, you may want to go for a bigger step, such as engaging in a conversation with someone you meet in a networking event and exchanging contact details.

Public speaking, which is often a great trigger for people with social anxiety, can also be a way to engage in exposure therapy. For example, you may want to join a public speaking group, such as a Meetup group, or a society in your university if you are studying. You don't need to start speaking in public right away, but you can slowly expose yourself to a group of people who do it without fear so you start associating public speaking with a positive emotion instead of an anxiety trigger. You can start small as well, such as by speaking with your friend, practicing a speech with your family, and so on. Or, if you struggle with authority figures, speaking to your boss about something you care about – your experience at work, a project you would like to work on, etc – is also a great option. The goal is to engage in activities that push you to try out things that would normally cause anxiety so you change your approach and feel more and more comfortable doing these things, anxiety-free.

If you work with a therapist, you might also engage in role-playing. This is where your therapist asks you to think about a situation that might be anxiety-inducing, such as speaking to a stranger, or even small situations like having to speak to a clerk at the grocery store. Or, your therapist may make you do the opposite by asking you to play the role of someone who is confident and assertive in social situations, and then practice social skills and techniques that can help you feel more comfortable and confident in real-life situations. If you do not have a therapist, this is also something that you can do on your own, in front of a mirror.

Exposure therapy is a scary experience for many people dealing with anxiety, but it works like a charm when executed successfully. Try it out and see if it works!

# Chapter Six: Mindfulness and Meditation

There is a growing body of work outlining the benefits of mindfulness and meditation on anxiety. The former is based on the idea that as meditation has been shown to reduce feelings of stress and to create new neural pathways due to the brain's neuroplasticity, it can also reduce feelings of anxiety by helping your brain learn new concepts. For example, mantra meditation, which is where you focus on specific sentences (e.g., "I am at peace" or "I am in control of my feelings") can help your brain internalize these thoughts, thereby reducing the impact that more negative thoughts, such as the ones mentioned in previous chapters, may have on you and your symptoms of anxiety.

Mindfulness is a form of meditation that invites you to focus on the present moment, and hence to forget about the other things that may be worrying you. While you perform a mindfulness exercise, you are encouraged to focus solely on the sensations you can feel in the present moment, thereby forcing you to stop overthinking and stop giving into thoughts pushed by your anxiety. You become increasingly aware of the present moment instead of considering what *could* happen in the future. Likewise, mindfulness and meditation alike encourage you to accept and respect yourself, which can help reduce self-judgment, as you learn to focus on the positive feelings you have and the positive thoughts you think. This can be powerful, especially if techniques like exposure therapy feel too extreme at first.

Of course, meditation is also well-known for being an exercise that reduces physical symptoms of anxiety as well as it invites us to calm our breathing and has remarkable calming effects. The more we meditate, the better we become at fostering these feelings of serenity. Then, the more skilled we become at using meditation throughout the day, particularly when we feel anxious. Therefore, meditation and mindfulness alike can be used when you feel very anxious, and they can be done in as little as 5 minutes, making this method excellent for those struggling with anxiety throughout the day (or generalized anxiety). Naturally, this is applicable to those with social phobia as well – simply try out meditation or mindfulness before an anxiety-inducing event, and see if it helps.

To incorporate mindfulness and meditation into your anxiety management routine, consider starting with small, manageable steps. A good way to do so is through the body scan exercise, where you sit in silence for as long as needed and imagine the stress and anxiety leaving your body, limb by limb. You can do this as many times as necessary to feel relief. Otherwise, you might start by practicing deep breathing for a few minutes each day, or by taking a short mindful walk in nature and focusing on the present moment – what can you see around you? How do the trees look? What color are the leaves? What does the air smell like? Pay attention to the small details and focus on those instead of giving into anxious thoughts.

# Chapter Seven:
## Social Skills Training

While the aforementioned methods work well for many people, you may need a different kind of method if you struggle with socializing in general. In such cases, social skills training can be particularly helpful. Social skills training is a type of therapy that can be effective in treating social anxiety. Since social anxiety can make it difficult for you to engage in social situations, social skills training can help you develop the **skills and confidence** you need to navigate social situations more effectively. For example, you might feel overwhelmed by a social situation if you are worried about what you will talk about. *How will I know what to say? How can I network with people I don't know? What if they judge me?* Social skills training comes in handy in these situations because it teaches you how to cope with these feelings by training you to handle all kinds of social situations.

Social skills training has a few steps, and it usually starts with goals. For this, you need to be ready to confront your social anxiety by accepting that it is a problem and it is causing distress in your everyday life, even if it is a tough admission! This goes back to the triggers we discussed earlier – what kind of triggers do you have? How do you want these to change? What would you like to feel like instead when you face those triggers? You might want to become more comfortable when meeting new people, when starting conversations, or you may want to learn how to assert your opinion without feeling like a panic attack is coming your way. There are all kinds of skills that you can learn, so start by pinpointing the areas you'd like to work on.

Then, the next step is to learn these skills. For example, if you have pinpointed that you struggle when needing to keep up eye contact, this may be one of the first skills you work on. This should ideally be done with a therapist, but you can do so with yourself and with friends or family members as well. You can let them know that you are working on this and that you'd appreciate their support. Otherwise, you may also want to work on using appropriate body language if this is something that worries you. You could learn skills like how to come up with questions to get the conversation going, or how to respond to questions when you do not know the answer, such as bouncing the ball back in the other's court, or how to divert a conversation. There are all kinds of skills you can learn, but it again goes back to what triggers you.

# Conclusion:
## Go Back to the Root

Throughout this book, we have looked at the various facets of social anxiety and the methods that you can employ to reduce the symptoms and gain back control. That being said, there is an important aspect to keep in mind: at the root of it, anxiety is often grounded in feelings of inadequacy, and negative self-talk fuelled by self-consciousness. As such, while the methods listed earlier will help you address the symptoms of your social anxiety, the real work begins with you. When facing your anxiety, try to pinpoint where this is coming from. Why do you feel this way about yourself? What tells you that you are not worth being listened to, that your thoughts and opinions are not valuable or not worth being considered as legitimate by others?

It all starts with you. Sometimes, the easiest way to start coping with social anxiety is to look inward and to change the way you speak to yourself. What if it were as simple as changing a thought like *"everyone's going to laugh at me, I'm going to embarrass myself"* to "*I haven't seen these people in a long time, I'm sure they'll be excited to see me. I should go!*"? Give it a try. Convince yourself! Negative self-talk is at the root of these feelings of anxiety, so take control over them and rewire the way your brain works. Tell yourself that you *are* worth being listened to, and change the narrative. Reframe those thoughts into more positive ones. Then, continue trying out the various methods outlined in this book and see which ones work best for you.

We are all different, so your reaction to some of these methods will greatly differ from other people's reactions to the same method. You may react very well to exposure therapy, or you may need more time to get used to the idea. Perhaps you can start with CBT worksheets, which you can do from the comfort of your own home and which can make you feel instantly more in control of the situation. Sometimes, simply asking yourself the question "*What evidence do I have for these fears and worries I feel?*" can lead you to reframe the situation entirely, realizing that you are only fuelling the avoidance-anxiety cycle. That's where you can truly start to break it.

I believe in you and your potential! Now, you need to believe in yourself too. Start small, even if it means just smiling at the clerk at the grocery store. Remember to congratulate yourself and to pat yourself on the back as you achieve new milestones. What is easy for one person may be extremely difficult for you, so every milestone achieved is one worth celebrating.

Your new life begins today.

Sincerely,
James Bennet